from inside Schrödinger's box

poems by

Cyan Orr

Finishing Line Press
Georgetown, Kentucky

from inside Schrödinger's box

For Bob,
for opening the box

With thanks to Andy,
for tending to so many almost-dead cats

Copyright © 2017 by Cyan Orr
ISBN 978-1-63534-238-3 First Edition
All rights reserved under International and Pan-American Copyright Conventions.
No part of this book may be reproduced in any manner whatsoever without written permission from the publisher, except in the case of brief quotations embodied in critical articles and reviews.

ACKNOWLEDGMENTS

Acknowledgements, in appreciation, to:

Switched-on-Gutenberg, first publishers of "Metacognition"
Spillway, first publishers of "Idaho" and
Mason's Road, first publishers of "The Scarecrow's Response"

Publisher: Leah Maines

Editor: Christen Kincaid

Cover Art: Robert Orr

Author Photo: Robert Orr

Cover Design: Elizabeth Maines McCleavy

Printed in the USA on acid-free paper.
Order online: www.finishinglinepress.com
also available on amazon.com

Author inquiries and mail orders:
Finishing Line Press
P. O. Box 1626
Georgetown, Kentucky 40324
U. S. A.

Table of Contents

Cat's Paw 1
Yellow Jacket 2
Clover Chain 3
Three Quarter Moon on Wet Grass 4
Bytes 5
Idaho 9
Water Color 10
The Cat's Bowl 11
Momentum 12
Grace 13
Infinities 14
Metacognition 17
Higher Intelligence 18
Trajectory 19
Factors of Ten 21
Open or Closed 22
I Do Believe 23
Hiberion 24
Tetragrammaton 25
The Scarecrow's Response 26
Morning Fodder 27
Toward Silence 28
Bonfire 29
This Old Cat 30
Garden 31
Germination 32
Transubstantiation 33
From Inside Schrödinger's Box 34

Cat's Paw

Whose game is this,
to box us in a finite time
in which the very air threatens poisoned

probabilities? We teeter
on the precipice of present-
mindedness

tasting today a honeysuckle wind,
flitting Monarch wings.
Tomorrow

a quantum guess, a leap
of faith in something
outside the mime's

felt box, solid as sense,
against the stolid desperation
of four blank walls closed

to all but
death and life,
and death.

The Yellow Jacket . . .

       like a helicopter parent
annoying with whizzing e-
mails and phone calls, driving
me to swat and swear, has landed

her striped butt, thorax, whatever
in my pineapple juice. She
splutters legs and wings
against the sweet ambrosia

muttering a waspish damn
at the free-winged gods who
landed her in this mess, drowning
in her own greedy

pleasure. In pity, I dump
the glass. She licks her
wings and breezes back
to natter against the gods.

Clover Chain

Cross-legged on the stoop—
june-warmed by waves of skin-smell, turned
earth, and feral grass—
the child plucks from the pile

another bloom. She loops
a stem around, through, ties off
the white clover head, bloom
after bloom, stem

after stem, deft fingers stitching
a stillness so deep
that the clattering of dishes
behind the ripped screen door,

the taunting of child laughter
in jump-rope rhythms across the street,
even the chortling of birds
make no conscious sound

but are woven into the lengthening chain
trailing down the rough grey steps,
twined and tangled,
clover stem

by clover stem by

Three Quarter Moon on Wet Grass

I want to catch you live, boxed
between my palms

passed to a jam jar, lid pierced
to sift the air, to sift the light,

but you fluoresce
your rhythm through a synapse

of star-beaded sky and bulging
moon that pulses

your alien voice and confounds
me again in the cryptic

cross of geist and grass.

Bytes

I. Last Seen

They found Don Domsky yesterday,
dead. His heart gave up

a year ago. His house
and yard looked beaten down as ever. The kitchen

roof had caved, the linoleum cracked,
but Donald's TV blared away. Neighbors

shook their heads. Cantankerous old coot.
Weeds grew. The mail

piled up. Everyone thought
old Don had gone to a home,

but when the policeman jimmied
the door, there he sat, settled

in his La-Z-boy, remote
in hand, watching the Giants

fumble a pass. If he hadn't already
died, Don would have damned

them all and changed the channel.

II. A Man

                in Chester, New Jersey beat
his 73-year-old wife to death

with a baseball bat—an old wooden Spalding
hung by its lip on a rack in the garage—

after 52 years of marriage he went
(how did he go? where

did he go?)
crazy. He thought she

was cheating on him, wearing
Rose Serenity L'Oreal

lipstick with a new silky swirl blouse
she'd splurged on at the Marshall's just

opened in August near Shop Rite. They
(his wife and son) had tried to cajole

him, the man, into seeing
someone—he'd been acting

a bit odd, suspicious and all—but no
one suspected he'd snap. The neighbors

shook their heads—such a shame, the Star
Ledger reported, they seemed

so happy together.

III. Inquiry

He hunched himself
into an old round-cornered Frigidaire, abandoned

on his parents' dusty porch. He knew
he'd fit. He'd just been stuffed

into his locker yesterday—again. His disappearance hit
the local news: "Missing student, brilliant, beloved by peers."

They discovered him days later, clutching
notebook and pen in stiffened fingers

bent to log his slowing
pulse, his fading apperception.

In neatly labeled columns, he'd made
his mark, measuring

his own asphyxiation. Five lines
before the shivering stream of ink

scrawled off the page

IV. Elevator

Suzanne Hart stepped into the open/
closed box on the 26th floor. The mechanism

malfunctioned, trapping
her lagging foot, racing her upward, half

in, half out. Freak accident,
said CBS News. The other twelve lifts remained

in service. The EMTs opened
the doors, unknowing,

but Suzanne
had already moved on.

Idaho

The old man whickers his way
down Jack Ass Creek through slush on the banks—
not the road, doesn't like the road—hocks
his pelts off on Avery Wellum, knows he'll claim them
as his own, and not poached neither,
crosses the Payette into Horseshoe Bend
where he stocks his pack at Kalac's grocery,
incomers staring, he sneers
as he wraps the tobacco in oilskin;
picks up a paper to pad his boots,
spits first on Obama's picture—
tips his felt to Miz Kalac,
stares down the sheriff
relieves himself on the post office wall,
chuckling
and tilts himself back
to freedom.

Water Color

This dabbled bridge across
the Siuslaw limned

with color and contrast, purples
and reds that ease to orange and gold,

this span over cyan ripples, footed
by daisies with sunbright centers

lends me its artist's eye with which to recast
those somber shadows that ghost

the corners of a silent
sunfall, or haunt the teardrops

of a too-gray dawn, playing them into a palette
of quizzical tints and tones. This eye, this ear,

this taste awash in a sensory
spectrum that has no science but

that of broken waves
prismed into joy.

The Cat's Bowl

is empty.
Someone ought to fill it.
The cat will be yowling soon,
pacing and glaring
with those green slotted eyes
like a lion caged,
restless, waiting.
One of those feeder things
might work,

for awhile
but when it was empty
someone would need to fill it.
If only they'd let the damned cat out
to hunt,
kill its own meat.
But no,
that's not civilized.
It's an indoor cat
declawed
with an empty bowl.

Momentum
    Tucumcari, New Mexico, 1963

We four kids—I am 8—are being herded down the heat-cracked sidewalk
along Route 66 from the Triple A guidebook family restaurant
back to the Best Western—a family vacation from California to Kansas City
in a desert dust Impala station wagon—
relieved to stretch along this short block even in the settling dusk heat
as the sun wilts into the horizon.
We squabbled the day away restless and queasy, now
none of us wants to be confined
in that claustrophobic double queen room, muted
earth tones carefully matched, with no space
to play, run, stretch, with a roll-away cot made up at the end of one of the beds
and the air conditioner whining ineffectually. I don't hear
the wheedling *hurry up, come on*
what's the problem now?
I am lagging, again,
I often lag—
and there it is, in the scrubby lot next to the motel, the battered
old cart, wooden slats loose and jagged, just another dusty skeleton
an hour ago, now
rears,
stark, black,
backlit by fire
gold-edged and flaming carnelian ribbons,
an iconic echo,
broken, and
abandoned.

Grace

Hip-sore from a cold night on hard ground, I roll
my sleeping bag toward the sun stream-

ing through the half-closed zipper. Clumsy
fingers open up the sting

and glory of a frosty dawn. Struggling
into wool and will, pulling

on scuffed boots, I clamber
out, newborn, into a kaleidoscope of hue that blinds

me from the task of pumping
the stove, filling the pan. My mittened

hands keep working while I drink a soulful
of mountain-vale ambrosia. Ice-blue water

from a rock-filtered stream aches
and fills me. The memory trace of yesterday's climb

in the slinging rain, switch-back after grey and muddy
switch-back, knots my legs—

I twist and stretch the sinews
of aching perseverance,

but here I stand, senses battered
and alive, wordless

Infinities

> $Aleph_{null}$—the infinity of counting numbers, 1, 2, 3....
> $Aleph_{one}$—the infinity of real numbers, perhaps $2^{Aleph_{null}}$
> $Aleph_{two}$—the next, conjectured infinity, $2^{Aleph_{one}}$?

$Aleph_{null}$

five-year-olds
in playground chants:

*Count higher than the swings, as high
as trees; I*

*can swing beyond the acorn
tops into the wooly sky*

*forever and for always
longer, higher. Can even*

God count so far? Can He,
the Great I Am, He

Who Is? I finger the reach
beyond the stretch

of cognizance
until there is only

an endless echo,
who is, who
is, who?

Aleph$_{one}$

Cantor sang his coded
score, trilling tones—

discounted by the rational,
oblations served ingenuously

to scholars whose doubts
increased

in winter's exponential leaps. Two
to the Aleph$_{null}$, stormed

in the gap
between the known

and wild conjecture,
his guess, like

snow deepening
in the pass, an immensity

of crystal flakes we shoe
across, and then discount.

Aleph_{two}

What neurons spark
this untamed

artistry that seizes
a mind from quiet

contemplation, daring
it to mold and sculpt

its own heretic
fantasy into the real?

Impelled,
we leave our constant

sorting—good from bad,
right from wrong, us from

them—to scrape away
the tacit veil of certainty

digging deep
into the medium of our doubt

and depth, uncovering
what will.

Metacognition

We are immersed, you
and I, in studying
the brain, dissecting
it, like a frog thinking
about being a frog, ribbits echoing
from ribbit centers in the left temporal
amphibial lobe while we cut
away layers of cortex—undulated
brain skin—over white
glial—ribbit—cells to uncover
with sharp and gentle
scalpels the limbic
drama, the hippocampal memory,
the internal lily pad system of myelinated
pathways searching with flicking
tongues for the bitter taste
of the essential.

Higher Intelligence

> *And one of the things that comes out of the Principle of Computational Equivalence is that there really can't be something special that is intelligence—it's all just computation.*
> —Steve Wolfram

If Wolfram
is correct and we are just

the product of some
iterative random code,

a simplicity that unfurls
into greater complexity like swarm

intelligence—an ant colony
whose pristine

mechanism is merely the tangled interplay
of individual ant-cogs turning

their step-lock programs into the type of intel
with which the NSA

is so infatuated—then we are neither
destroying ourselves nor

our simplistic world, or maybe
we raze both—it's entropy,

no worries—but god
help the guy who wrote

the code and left us
aching, ravenous to touch

the brink of holiness

Trajectory
    for Dr. L

I'm writing by flashlight, waiting for the sun,
considering,
why does a poet bother to teach math?

You write and read—incognizant—
still stuck on the $\sqrt{-17}$
as if "imaginary" meant "no imagination."

But what if, like every miracle,
this taming of a flaming ball to rise—
on cue—
sketching silhouettes of trees,
coloring the wavelengths of the sky
from black to gold, pink, starburst-orange,
settling to blue,
is a metaphor,
an excellent metaphor,
worthy of a poem.

Like your not-yet-born child,
already kicking and sucking her thumb
unaware of the knitting of neuron chains,
woven from the curled ribbon
of her dna
whose fractal coding forms those tiny fingernails
you'll have to trim,
we sense.
But do we see?

We labor too long, sometimes,
over the birth of a poem,
forgetting its conception,
forgetting the *mathematics* whose dense encryption builds
to that unbearable climax that bursts
into the analogy of a child.
And then, like proud new dads showing pictures
and shaking hands, we sketch,
in vivid tones, a description
of the metaphor.

You find mathematics
prosaic,
but is it really less poetic to trace the template
of the magical?
less passionate to hear the rhythm of your lust and love echoed
in the heartbeat of your child?

This flashlight
(its imagery created by some poet
whose equations made electrons into stars) dims
in the glory of that solar edge.
Light and warmth shoot, vector-like, to earth penetrating
the fertile soil of her imagination.

The sun flares, a glorious re-
solution, and here I am
still writing, flashlight off, considering…

Factors of Ten

In this body—bone and bulk—
the specialization of cells is directed
by dna guilds

developing each peculiar craft
and art toward the survival
of a complexity twined

together, igniting first
into life itself, then
into mind and mind-

fullness, but
the cells that articulate
this thumb to clasp

another hand, to caress
a thigh
are neither conscious

of self, nor conscious
of mind:
their mind-self wallows in a distant lobe of sardine-packed

neurons unknotted, synapse by synapse, leaving these dark
to its pleasure
so how will we know

when the interweaving of global
lives, of person-cells joined by fiber
optic nerves across orbital chasms

will spark a spectacular mega-
mind of which we
are only sinew and skin, twitching,

clutching one another to ensure
breath to a body of whom
we are not aware.

Open or Closed

                —it matters
to the cat. He is, after all, the sphinx

of quantum certainty. He channels
the spirit dead and resurrects

reality, such as it is, from the waste
basin of particle physics. But,

did Schrödinger ever really
own a cat? What magnetism conjured

his any-cat into this bounded space?
What gravity compels retracted claws

and silences the yowls? God knows
no scientist could miss the evidence

if this tabby's still alive.

I do believe

                    in trolls
and hook-nosed witches
who poison the fruit

of everyday. I've seen
their mirrored jealousies,
in our reflections, but

though I am haunted
by the melancholy of dwarves
digging, ever digging,

I still believe
in fairy-angels sprinkling
a mystic holiness
in the muggy hot-June dark.

Hiberion

…in this dead time,
arthritic finger branches bare

and vulnerable, pointing
to a mourning

sky, white silken
snow-shroud wrapping

houses, roads, the needles
on the firs, smothering

the question—I think,
therefore—the myth of spring-

ing up again to
        breathe
        bloom
        be—

I am, I
am.

Tetragrammaton

My brain is not elastic enough
to encounter eleven quantum
dimensions, to imagine black holes,
or envision dark matter. I count on the sunrise
to set, knowing in some intellectual tunnel
of nerves that we circle it, not vice-
versa, but wondering how Galileo knew
he wasn't the center when I can't really conceive
of being anything less. I know there are other livable
planets and yet there are bigger mysteries here,
in the scatter of so many disparate human
faces across the span of earth's continents. Our
miniscule lives, beaten out in poverty or wealth, crawling through histories
of eking existence make no sense if we
are merely bacteria, infecting
our world, lush and sere, verdant and desert, with the fall
of Adam and the blaze of reincarnated glory. How can
we know what to believe in the taunting weave
of mythologies and magic that lead us, somehow,
to kindness and holiness as right,
and ungraspable. We are offended
by the pain we cause one another, and so
name it bigger than our wants, *it is out of love,*
it is for religion, it is for the best. If it
were only chance that niggled us from
our one-celled beginnings, then I would guess
that the odds on evil are 50-50, and yet
we still vote for niceness, and
the crisscross hashes of Whoever's counting
make a pattern too mathematical,
too precise to be anything less than intentional, so,
though I am too small to intuit a theology
large enough, I keep losing myself
in a leap so vast it can neither be named,
or spoken, and yet,
and yet, it is.

The Scarecrow's Response
after Wallace Stevens

Ears stuffed
against a wailing wind
the scarecrow (without his brain)

sets crayon eyes on the tufted tips
of Kansas wheat, bowing,
beneath an unmarred yellow-gray sky

to the undifferentiated horizon
and being mindless sees
plains, and nothing

more. He hangs on, still,
mindfully empty, until
defenseless

he finds himself
whisking away
wistfulness to fashion,

to fire, *ex nihilo,*
straw dreams of wizards
and wit

Morning Fodder

Back steps slick with ice
on this no-moon morning, the porch
light sweeps away

a few feet of blackness
before giving out,
giving up. The trees shiver,

scuttling ice slivers.
Cold blisters through the hole
in my glove. The goats

mewl, willing me
through the piled
drifts. Chopping and scooping

the crusted snow, I open up
a path to the chain-link
gate. I push

hay into the rack, pour
feed, dump another ice cylinder
from the water bin, refill

it from the pump. The does shove
and butt, playing,
but Lucky, my wether, nuzzles close,

watches with me, patient, still, until
first light, spilling
fills the hungry dawn.

Toward Silence

> *And after the earthquake a fire; but the LORD was not in the fire: and after the fire a still silent voice. 1 Kings 19:12*

The Santa Anas whip across the basin,
whisking away the L.A. smog,
scouring the ugliness from the skies.

As they rush, silent and furious,
I, too, am scrubbed clean
as no atonement from behind the hiss
of a sliding screen ever made me.
That quavering voice muttering Latin sibilants
may have had the power,
but those strange whispers never touched me.

Skittering leaf and trembling branch
are my icons for the infinite,
incarnate evidence as heretical as any other.
So be it.
The stirring of this wind
is that which I cannot understand.
but beyond, below, beneath
soughs the still and quiet voice.

You pray for me aloud
and tongue the gospel of your certainty
in words you've uttered skyward.
I envy your salvation,

but I can only hear
the hushing of ancient trees,
bowing,
and breathe my inarticulate longing
toward silence.

Bonfire

Dusk drapes the flickering
of the burning brush, filling

the shadows, gloving
the reaching fingers of heat. Others,

easy companions,
pierce marshmallows with willow sticks,

char them, eat them anyway. Clumsily, I
settle on the edge

wrapped by cool dark, I trace the kinetic
tuck and tip of flames. Their chatter

stills to a lonely hush and I am captured
by the cavern of an empty

sky poked with star-holes that draw
me away, invisible, unfindable

until foreign voices, calling,
shake me back to the chilled

damp air, to awkward alliances, to home,
to bed, to dream

of flame against dark
igniting an ember otherness.

This Old Cat

                    skulks, stiff-
legged now with years

and long-past hunts, eyes
less feral, the moon-gleam

lost, content to feed
indoors, giving space

to couching
this simplicity. Why

do we accept, at last,
this kenneling

just before the gas
ignites, the poison bursts,

and we discover, final-
ly, the way outside the box?

Garden
for Pat, in memory

I'd like to sit, robed and shaved, at the feet
of the Dalai Lama or any other current

hero-saint, awed and humbled in the hush
of whispered wisdom. Empty, I'd fill myself with guided

certainty and stent away the doubts that block
my faith, like the tumor in your colon—

so much waste.
Why are we stunned by looming death

as if the Path had ever changed? But even Christ,
knowing, knelt and begged. This bitter taste

will neither pass, nor last.
There is no other walk

and I am bowed by each unanswered prayer.

Germination

We are mesmerized,
each spring, by broken seed casings—cocoons

cast aside to spawn foreign forms
as if water, light, earth were not joined

to this zygotic spark in a necessary unity. It is
not the seed which blooms into blade

and bud, rather form and energy enfold
the bigger resurrection born of pain, of broken-

ness. We imagine dimensions
caged by our own awareness as if

the slumbering larva was anointed
with a vision of its patterned someday wings;

we vegetate, like packaged kernels, in a coma
so incomprehensible we name it life

and mourn its passing, but until the envelope
is torn and spilled, flushed with catastrophic

floods, burned with a holy incandescence, we lie,
sere and barren, waiting

Transubstantiation

Annie slides
her skinny legs between
the pews, stills her wriggling
feet, hushed into the candled dusk,
peopled emptiness,
the church is full
of rustled creaks and the too-sweet taste
of Givenchy scent on Sunday
clothes. She eases away the solemn
kyrie eleison, modulated to maximize
contrition, breathing in-
stead the ghost
of a giddy vastness that was
and is, and roils her with its
Presence
so she is neither child
nor saint but only
in and of the space between
her templed hands.

From inside Schrödinger's Box

I have only
this particularity—this diamond leaf
that dulls and flares
with passing clouds,

this streaked window peering.
I have only
this worn chair tilting
toward the whorls

and grains of my familiar
space, tilled with tokens—square clock,
use-worn books, tossed pens—to grant
my ownership and still

the world respires
its flux and flow and
I am only
held by happenstance

and probability. A begonia
blooms outside, this day, this
hour, efflorescent as it dies,
petal to gloom,

earth-bound like my
self, my skin, the glaze
that shrouds
my imagination.

I have only
this make-shift habitation
from which to spark the wondering
sense that pricks
and burns and fires
me to guess what
lies outside the certainty
that here I am, alive.

Cyan Orr was born in Akron Ohio. She served as an educator at various schools on the east and west coast, teaching Mathematics and Psychology, primarily on the high school level. She held the position of partner in the Windward Learning Center, a tutoring center focusing on mathematics and test preparation for middle and high school students. Her undergraduate degree is in Mathematics and Psychology, earned at the University of Redlands. She also holds a Master of Arts degree in Counseling from Azusa Pacific University and a Master of Fine arts degree in Creative Writing from Ashland University. She has published poetry in the journals *Spillway, Switched-on-Gutenberg,* and *Mason's Road*. She serves on the planning committee for the Big Wave Poetry Festival in Florence, Oregon. In addition to her poetry, Cyan has written a mathematics text, *Building Numbers*, which she has used with high school students to creatively uncover the structures of the Real number system and to explore its idiosyncrasies.

Cyan is the mother of two children. She lives on the Oregon coast with her husband Bob, a cat, a dog and a rabbit.

www.ingramcontent.com/pod-product-compliance
Lightning Source LLC
LaVergne TN
LVHW041505070426
835507LV00012B/1344